Table of Contents

Introduction.. 1
Chapter 1: Introduction to Freelancing................ 5
Chapter 2: Identifying Your Freelancing Niche.. 9
Chapter 3: Building Your Freelancing Brand... 14
Chapter 4: Setting Up Your Freelancing Business.. 19
Chapter 5: Finding Freelancing Clients............ 24
Chapter 6: Pricing Your Freelance Services.... 29
Chapter 7: Managing Freelance Projects......... 35
Chapter 8: Delivering High-Quality Freelance Work... 40
Chapter 9: Building Client Relationships and Generating Referrals... 44
Chapter 10: Scaling Your Freelancing Business. 49

Introduction

Welcome to "The Ultimate Guide on How to Start a Freelancing Business!" In this book, we're going to dive into the fascinating world of freelancing and equip you with invaluable insights and practical tips to launch and grow a successful freelancing career.

Embracing the Freelance Lifestyle

Freelancing has emerged as a popular and viable career path for many entrepreneurs who seek control over their professional lives. Whether you're a writer, designer, developer, marketer, or any other professional, freelancing offers the freedom to work on your terms and choose projects that ignite your passion.

In this introductory chapter, we'll take a closer look at the concept of freelancing and the myriad advantages it brings. We'll also explore the evolving landscape of work and understand why freelancing has become such an attractive option for many aspiring entrepreneurs.

The Rise of Freelancing

Over the years, traditional employment models have undergone significant changes. Technological advancements and globalization have revolutionized the way we work, making the conventional 9-to-5 office job just one of many options.

Freelancing has gained tremendous momentum as more professionals seek autonomy, flexibility, and the opportunity to pursue projects they are genuinely passionate about. This shift in mindset has fostered a thriving freelance market, connecting talented individuals with businesses in need of their skills.

Today, freelancers can collaborate with clients worldwide, work remotely, and enjoy the freedom to set their own schedules and rates. The rise of online platforms and digital marketplaces has further simplified the process of finding freelance opportunities and establishing a successful business.

The Advantages of Freelancing

Freelancing offers a host of benefits for entrepreneurs looking to start their own businesses. Let's delve into some of the key advantages:

Flexibility
One of the most enticing aspects of freelancing is the unparalleled flexibility it provides. As a freelancer, you have the liberty to choose when and where you work. This flexibility allows you to create a schedule that suits your lifestyle, enabling you to pursue other interests, spend

quality time with family, or even travel while earning a living.

Increased Earning Potential

Unlike traditional jobs where your income is often capped by a fixed salary or hourly rate, freelancing empowers you to set your own prices and take on multiple clients simultaneously. By leveraging your skills and expertise, you can potentially earn more as a freelancer compared to a traditional employment setup.

Work-Life Balance

Freelancing offers the opportunity to achieve a better work-life balance. You can prioritize activities outside of work, whether it's spending time with loved ones, engaging in hobbies, or attending to personal responsibilities. With effective time management, you can design a lifestyle that harmonizes with both your personal and professional goals.

Career Growth

As a freelancer, you have the freedom to select projects and clients that align with your interests and aspirations. This autonomy allows you to continuously develop your skills and expand your expertise in areas that truly excite you. This focus on professional growth can lead to increased opportunities and help you become a sought-after expert in your industry.

What's Next?

Now that we've explored the rise of freelancing and the numerous benefits it offers, it's time to delve deeper into the world of freelancing and understand how to identify your niche. In the next chapter, we'll discuss the importance of finding your freelancing niche and how it can help you stand out in a competitive market.

Stay tuned, and let's embark on this exciting journey together!

Chapter 1: Introduction to Freelancing

Freelancing has seen a significant surge in popularity in recent years, transforming the traditional work landscape and creating fresh opportunities for entrepreneurs. In this chapter, we'll delve into the concept of freelancing, explore its advantages, and discuss why it has become such a viable career option.

Exploring the Concept of Freelancing and Its Advantages

Freelancing is a work arrangement where individuals offer their skills and services to multiple clients on a project-by-project basis, rather than being tied to a single employer. This setup provides freelancers with greater control over their work and a higher degree of autonomy.

One of the standout benefits of freelancing is the ability to work with clients from around the globe. Thanks to technological advancements and the internet, freelancers can collaborate remotely and deliver their services without being limited by geographic boundaries. This opens up a vast array of opportunities and significantly expands the potential client pool.

Another significant advantage is the flexibility

that freelancing offers. Freelancers have the freedom to choose their own working hours, select projects that align with their interests and skills, and work from virtually anywhere. This flexibility allows individuals to create a work-life balance that suits their needs and preferences, which is often difficult to achieve in traditional employment settings.

Moreover, freelancing presents the potential for increased earnings. As a freelancer, you can set your own rates and negotiate with clients based on the value you provide. Unlike traditional employment, where your income is typically capped by a fixed salary, freelancing allows you to earn more by taking on multiple projects and building a portfolio of satisfied clients.

The Rise of Freelancing as a Career Option

The traditional work environment has undergone significant changes, contributing to the rise of freelancing as a legitimate career path. Many people are now seeking the independence and ability to pursue their passions by starting their own freelancing ventures.

Several factors have contributed to the rise of freelancing. First, technological advancements have made remote collaboration and communication more accessible than ever. Freelancers can seamlessly work with clients and colleagues from different parts of the world using tools like video conferencing, project management software, and cloud-based storage solutions.

Additionally, there is a growing demand for specialized skills and expertise, creating niches that freelancers can fill. Businesses and individuals often need specific services that can be efficiently provided by freelancers with specialized knowledge in particular fields. This demand has led to an increase in freelance opportunities across various industries.

The desire for a better work-life balance and a more fulfilling career has also fueled the growth of freelancing. Many individuals no longer wish to be confined to a traditional 9-to-5 job and are seeking greater freedom and flexibility in their work. Freelancing allows them to choose projects that align with their personal interests and passions, leading to a more satisfying career path.

In the next chapter, we will delve into the importance of identifying your freelancing niche and how to effectively stand out in a competitive market. By specializing in a specific area, freelancers can differentiate themselves and attract high-paying clients. Stay tuned for valuable insights and strategies on finding your freelancing niche.

Chapter 2: Identifying Your Freelancing Niche

Choosing a specific niche in freelancing is a crucial step toward achieving success as a freelancer. By identifying and specializing in a particular area, you can position yourself as an expert in your field and attract high-quality clients. In this chapter, we will explore the importance of finding your freelancing niche and standing out in a competitive market.

Understanding the Importance of a Niche

When you first start your freelancing journey, it might seem like a good idea to offer a wide range of services to appeal to as many potential clients as possible. However, trying to be a jack of all trades often makes it difficult to stand out in a crowded marketplace. Instead, narrowing down your focus and becoming an expert in a specific niche allows you to differentiate yourself and attract clients who are looking for specialized skills.

Identifying a niche enables you to leverage your unique expertise, experiences, and interests. This not only sets you apart from your competition but also makes it easier for clients to find you. When clients search for freelancers, they often look for specialists who have a deep understanding of their industry or specific project requirements.

Identifying Your Strengths and Passions

To identify your freelancing niche, start by assessing your strengths, skills, and passions. Ask yourself:

- What are you truly passionate about?
- What skills do you excel in?
- What past experiences or qualifications can you leverage in your freelance work?

Reflect on your professional background and expertise. Think about the skills you have developed throughout your career and identify the areas where you shine. It could be graphic design, web development, writing, marketing, photography, or any other skill set you have honed over time. Choose a niche that aligns with your expertise and passion to maximize your chances of success.

Additionally, it's essential to stay updated with the latest industry trends and advancements. By continuously learning and keeping up with industry changes, you can position yourself as a knowledgeable and reliable freelancer within your niche.

Researching the Market

Once you have identified your strengths and passions, the next step is to research the market. Look for demand in your chosen niche and assess the competition. Are there already many freelancers offering similar services? How saturated is the market?

Start by identifying potential clients and target markets within your niche. Conduct market research to understand their needs, pain points, and preferences. This will help you tailor your services to meet their specific requirements and differentiate yourself from competitors. Consider reaching out to professionals or businesses within your target market to gain insights into the challenges they face and how you can provide valuable solutions. Networking with industry experts can also open doors to collaborations and referrals.

Branding Yourself as a Specialist

Once you have identified your freelancing niche, it's crucial to establish yourself as a specialist in that area. Develop a strong personal brand that highlights your expertise, professionalism, and unique value proposition. This includes creating a compelling portfolio, showcasing your work, and optimizing your online presence.

Craft a clear and concise elevator pitch that clearly communicates your niche, the value you offer, and what sets you apart from the competition. Tailor your marketing materials, website, and social media profiles to reflect your niche and target market. Take advantage of content marketing to establish yourself as an authority in your niche. Create and share valuable content, such as blog posts, e-books, or videos, that provide insights and solutions relevant to your target audience. This will not only attract potential clients but also build trust and credibility in your field.

Conclusion

Identifying your freelancing niche is a crucial step toward building a successful freelance business. By specializing in a specific area, you can position yourself as an expert, attract high-quality clients, and stand out in a competitive market. Take the time to assess your strengths and passions, research the market, and brand yourself as a specialist. In the next chapter, we will focus on building your freelancing brand to further differentiate yourself and attract your ideal clients.

Chapter 3: Building Your Freelancing Brand

Creating a strong brand is crucial for freelancers who want to distinguish themselves in a competitive market and attract top-notch clients. Your brand represents your professional identity, setting you apart from other freelancers offering similar services. In this chapter, we'll delve into the key steps for building a successful freelancing brand.

Why Building Your Brand Matters

Think of your brand as the personality of your business. It gives potential clients an impression of who you are and what you offer. A strong brand not only attracts the right clients but also allows you to command higher rates for your services. Here are a few reasons why building your freelancing brand matters:

Differentiation:
In a crowded market, having a unique brand helps you stand out. By defining your niche and positioning yourself as an expert in that field, you can differentiate yourself from other freelancers. This makes you the go-to person for clients seeking specific services.

Client Trust and Credibility:
A well-established brand builds trust and

credibility with clients. When you consistently deliver high-quality work and project a professional image, clients are more likely to trust you with their projects and refer you to others.

Attracting High-Quality Clients:
A strong brand attracts clients who align with your values and appreciate your expertise. When you clearly communicate your unique value proposition and target the right audience, you attract clients who value your skills and are willing to pay a premium for your services.

Defining Your Brand Identity

To build a strong freelancing brand, you need to define your brand identity. This includes the visual elements, messaging, and values that represent your business. Here are some essential steps to defining your brand identity:

Identify Your Target Audience:
Understanding your target audience is crucial for creating a brand that resonates with potential clients. Research the market and identify your ideal clients' demographics, preferences, and pain points. Tailor your brand messaging to address their needs and position yourself as the solution to their problems.

Create a Consistent Visual Identity:
Consistency in your visual identity helps create

a strong brand presence. Design a professional logo, choose a color palette that reflects your brand personality, and create branded templates for your website, social media profiles, and marketing materials. Ensure all your visual elements are consistent across different platforms to create a recognizable brand identity.

Craft Your Brand Story:
Your brand story is the narrative that communicates your values, mission, and unique selling proposition. It helps clients connect with your brand on a deeper level. Craft a compelling brand story that showcases your expertise, passion, and the problems you solve for your clients.

Develop a Strong Online Presence:
In today's digital age, having a robust online presence is essential for building your freelancing brand. Create a professional website that showcases your portfolio, testimonials, and contact information. Utilize social media platforms to engage with your target audience and share valuable content related to your niche. Remember to maintain a consistent brand voice and messaging across all online channels.

Building Your Brand Reputation

Establishing a strong brand reputation is vital

for attracting clients and growing your freelancing business. Here are some strategies to enhance your brand reputation:

Deliver Exceptional Work:
Consistently delivering high-quality work is the foundation of a strong brand reputation. Exceed client expectations, meet deadlines, and ensure open communication throughout the project. Happy clients will not only become repeat customers but also refer you to others, helping grow your brand reputation.

Cultivate Client Relationships:
Building strong relationships with your clients fosters loyalty and trust. Take the time to understand their needs, communicate effectively, and provide outstanding customer service. Going above and beyond for your clients will help create a positive brand reputation.

Solicit Testimonials and Reviews:
Testimonials and reviews are powerful tools for building your brand reputation. Ask satisfied clients for testimonials and encourage them to share their positive experiences on platforms like LinkedIn, Google Business, or your website. Positive reviews serve as social proof, attracting more clients to your freelancing business.

Network and Collaborate:

Networking with industry professionals and collaborating on projects helps build your brand reputation. Attend industry conferences, join online communities, and participate in relevant forums. Establishing connections and showcasing your expertise to a wider audience can significantly enhance your brand reputation.

Conclusion

Building your freelancing brand is essential for standing out in a competitive market and attracting high-quality clients. By defining your brand identity, crafting a compelling brand story, and delivering exceptional work, you can build a strong brand reputation and position yourself as an expert in your niche. In the next chapter, we will explore the key steps in setting up your freelancing business.

Chapter 4: Setting Up Your Freelancing Business

Setting up your freelancing business is a crucial step toward establishing yourself as a professional and ensuring your success in the freelancing world. This chapter explores the key elements involved in setting up your freelancing business and provides practical tips to help you get started on the right foot.

Determining Your Business Structure

Before diving into the setup of your freelancing business, it's important to determine the legal structure that best suits your needs. You have several options, including operating as a sole proprietorship, forming a limited liability company (LLC), or establishing a corporation. Each structure has its advantages and considerations. Consulting with a legal professional or accountant is recommended to make an informed decision.

Registering Your Business

Once you have decided on the business structure, the next step is to register your business. The specific requirements and processes may vary depending on your location, so it's essential to research and comply with the regulations and tax obligations in your country or region. Registering your business not only gives you legal protection but also adds credibility and professionalism to your freelancing venture.

Setting Up a Business Bank Account

Separating your personal and business finances is crucial for managing your freelancing business effectively. Open a separate bank account dedicated to your freelancing income and expenses. This will make it easier to track your business finances, ensure proper record-keeping, and simplify tax filing.

Obtaining Necessary Permits and Licenses

Depending on your industry and location, you may need to obtain certain permits or licenses to legally operate your freelancing business. Research the requirements and regulations specific to your niche and comply with any necessary permits or licenses. This will help you avoid legal issues and demonstrate professionalism to your clients.

Establishing an Accounting System

Maintaining accurate financial records is crucial for the success of your freelancing business. Establish an accounting system that works for you, whether through accounting software, spreadsheets, or hiring an accountant. Track your income, expenses, invoices, and taxes to stay organized and make informed business decisions.

Creating a Professional Website

In today's digital age, having a professional website is essential for promoting your freelancing business and attracting clients. Your website should showcase your services, portfolio, testimonials, and contact information. Invest in a clean and user-friendly design that reflects your brand and aligns with your target audience. Optimize your website for search engines to increase your online visibility and reach.

Setting Your Freelancing Rates

Determining your freelancing rates is an important step in setting up your business. Research industry standards, consider your experience and expertise, and assess the value you provide to clients. Be mindful of the market and the competition while also ensuring that your rates reflect your worth. Remember, it is okay to adjust your rates as you gain more experience and build a strong reputation.

Creating Contracts and Policies

Protecting yourself and your clients is crucial in freelancing. Create clear and comprehensive contracts that outline the scope of work, payment terms, deadlines, and any other relevant details. Consider consulting with a legal professional to ensure that your contracts are legally binding and provide sufficient protection. Additionally, establish policies regarding revisions, cancellations, and confidentiality to manage expectations and avoid misunderstandings.

Setting Up Your Workspace

Designating a dedicated workspace within your home or renting a coworking space can greatly contribute to your productivity and professionalism. Create a workspace that is comfortable, organized, and conducive to your work style. Invest in the necessary equipment and tools to support your freelancing business, such as a reliable computer, software, and other relevant technology.

Conclusion

Taking the time to set up your freelancing business properly will lay a strong foundation for your success. By determining your business structure, registering your business, setting up a dedicated bank account, obtaining necessary permits and licenses, establishing an accounting system, creating a professional website, setting your freelancing rates, creating contracts and policies, and setting up your workspace, you will be well-prepared to embark on your freelancing journey.

Chapter 5: Finding Freelancing Clients

Starting a freelancing business is an exciting venture, but one of the biggest challenges you'll face is finding a steady stream of clients. It might seem overwhelming at first, but with the right strategies and techniques, you can attract quality clients who appreciate and value your services. In this chapter, we'll dive into various methods to find freelancing clients and build a robust client base.

Define Your Target Audience

Before you begin your search for clients, it's crucial to define your target audience. Understanding who your ideal clients are will help you focus your marketing efforts more effectively. Consider factors such as the industry they operate in, their location, the size of their company, and their specific needs or pain points. By having a clear picture of your target audience, you'll be better equipped to attract clients who are the perfect fit for your services.

Utilize Online Platforms

One of the most effective ways to find freelancing clients is by utilizing online platforms. There are numerous websites that connect freelancers with clients across various industries. Popular freelancing platforms like Upwork, Freelancer, and Fiverr allow you to create a profile, showcase your skills and previous work, and bid on projects. These platforms are excellent starting points for building your client base.

In addition to freelancing platforms, social media can also be a valuable tool for finding clients. Create a professional profile on LinkedIn, Twitter, or other relevant social media sites, and actively engage with potential clients in your target industry. Join groups or communities related to your field, share valuable content, and network with industry professionals. Social media can help you establish your presence and attract clients who are interested in your services.

Leverage Your Network

Networking is a powerful way to find freelancing clients. Reach out to your existing network, which includes friends, family, former colleagues, and previous clients. Let them know about your freelancing services, as they might have connections or know someone in need of your expertise. Attend networking events, industry conferences, and join online communities where you can meet potential clients and build relationships.

Create a Compelling Portfolio

A well-crafted portfolio is essential for showcasing your previous work and attracting clients. Create a portfolio that highlights your best projects and demonstrates your skills and expertise. Include case studies, testimonials, and results achieved for previous clients. A well-organized and visually appealing portfolio will impress potential clients and help you stand out from other freelancers.

Cold Pitching

Cold pitching can be a highly effective way to find clients, although it requires some effort and perseverance. Identify potential clients that match your target audience and reach out to them with a personalized pitch. Research their business or industry beforehand and tailor your pitch to address their specific needs or pain points. Be concise, clear, and show how your services can solve their problems or help them achieve their goals. Cold pitching, when done correctly, can open doors to new opportunities.

Collaborate with Other Freelancers

Collaborating with other freelancers can lead to new clients and projects. Reach out to freelancers in complementary industries or those who share a similar target audience, and explore opportunities for collaboration. This can include partnering on projects, referring clients to each other, or even offering bundled services. By working together, you can leverage each other's networks and skills, ultimately expanding your client base.

Offer Value Through Content Marketing

Content marketing is another effective strategy for attracting freelancing clients. Create and share valuable content through blog posts, videos, podcasts, or social media. Provide insights, solutions, and helpful information related to your niche. By positioning yourself as an expert in your field, you'll attract potential clients who are looking for your expertise. Content marketing helps you build credibility and trust with your audience, making it more likely that they will choose your services when they need them.

Conclusion

Finding freelancing clients requires a proactive approach and a combination of various strategies. By defining your target audience, utilizing online platforms, networking, creating a compelling portfolio, cold pitching, collaborating with other freelancers, and offering value through content marketing, you can attract high-quality clients who value your services. Stay persistent and continuously refine your approach to ensure a steady stream of clients for your freelancing business. Remember, building a successful freelancing career takes time and effort, but with the right strategies, you can achieve your goals and thrive in the freelancing world.

Chapter 6: Pricing Your Freelance Services

Setting the right price for your freelance services is crucial for the success of your business. If your rates are too low, you risk undervaluing your work and compromising your profitability. On the other hand, if your rates are too high, you might deter potential clients. In this chapter, we'll explore various factors to consider when setting your freelance rates and strategies to ensure you're charging what you're worth.

Understanding the Value of Your Services

Before you can determine the right pricing structure, it's essential to understand the value you provide to your clients. Consider the following factors:

1. Expertise and Experience:
Your level of expertise and industry experience play a significant role in determining your value as a freelancer. Clients are often willing to pay a premium for professionals who can deliver high-quality work based on their knowledge and experience.

2. Specialized Skills:
If you possess specialized skills or offer niche

services that are in high demand, you can charge higher rates. Clients frequently seek experts who can deliver exceptional results in specific areas.

3. Time and Effort:
Consider the amount of time and effort required to complete a project. Projects that demand extensive research, complex problem-solving, or long working hours warrant higher rates.

Factors to Consider When Pricing Your Services

1. Market Rates:
Research the market rates within your industry and niche to understand the average pricing for similar services. This gives you a benchmark to ensure your rates are competitive.

2. Cost of Living and Overhead Expenses:
Take into account your cost of living and business expenses when setting your rates. Calculate your overhead costs, including software subscriptions, equipment, and business insurance. It's important to cover all your expenses and maintain profitability.

3. Demand and Supply:
Evaluate the demand for your services and assess the level of competition in your niche. If there's high demand and low supply, you can increase your rates. Conversely, if the market

is saturated with freelancers offering similar services, you may need to adjust your pricing accordingly.

4. Project Scope and Complexity:
Consider the scope and complexity of each project. Projects requiring additional research, revisions, meetings, or tight deadlines may warrant higher rates.

5. Client Budget:
Understand your target clients' budget and their willingness to invest in quality work. A client with a larger budget may be more willing to pay higher rates for top-notch services.

Strategies for Pricing Your Services

1. Hourly Rates:
One common approach is to charge an hourly rate. Calculate your desired annual income and expenses, and divide it by the number of billable hours per year. This gives you a starting point for your hourly rate. However, hourly rates may not be suitable for all projects and can limit your earning potential.

2. Project-Based Pricing:
Consider pricing your services based on the project scope and deliverables. Break down the project into specific milestones and quote a fixed price for each stage. This allows you to provide a transparent pricing structure to

clients and ensures you're adequately compensated for your work.

3. Value-Based Pricing:
With value-based pricing, you align your rates with the value you provide to the client. Instead of solely considering the time and effort invested, focus on the impact and results your work will generate. This approach often allows for higher earning potential as it recognizes the value you bring to the table.

4. Retainer Agreements:
Offer retainer agreements to clients who require ongoing support or regular work. This involves charging a fixed monthly fee for a set number of hours or specific services. Retainer agreements provide stability and guaranteed income while fostering long-term client relationships.

Communicating Your Pricing to Clients

When discussing pricing with clients, it's important to effectively communicate the value they will receive for their investment. Here are some tips:

1. Provide Detailed Breakdowns:
Break down your pricing to clearly communicate what the client will receive for their investment. Specify the deliverables,

timelines, and any additional services included in your quote.

2. Showcase Past Successes:
Highlight previous projects where you achieved exceptional results for clients. Sharing success stories and positive client testimonials can justify your pricing and demonstrate the value you bring.

3. Educate on the ROI:
Explain how your services will contribute to the client's return on investment (ROI). Help them understand how your work will impact their business growth, revenue, or efficiency.

4. Be Confident:
Confidence is key when discussing pricing with clients. Know your worth and articulate the value you offer. Clients are more likely to accept higher rates if they perceive you as a confident and competent professional.

Regularly Evaluate and Adjust Your Pricing

Remember, pricing isn't set in stone and should be evaluated regularly. Assess market trends, your competition, and your own business goals. If you find that your rates are no longer sustainable or competitive, be prepared to adjust them accordingly.

In Conclusion

Pricing your freelance services requires a balance between your expertise, market rates, and the value you provide to clients. By considering these factors and employing effective pricing strategies, you can ensure you're earning what you deserve while attracting high-quality clients who appreciate your work. Next, in Chapter 7, we will delve into managing freelance projects effectively to ensure success and client satisfaction.

Chapter 7: Managing Freelance Projects

As a freelancer, managing your projects effectively is essential for success. It's not just about completing the work within the agreed-upon deadline but also ensuring that you meet or exceed your client's expectations. In this chapter, we'll explore valuable insights and strategies to help you manage your freelance projects successfully.

Understanding Project Management

Project management is the process of planning, organizing, and controlling all the activities needed to complete a project. As a freelancer, adopting project management principles will help you stay organized, meet deadlines, maintain client satisfaction, and deliver high-quality work consistently.

Key Elements of Project Management for Freelancers

Let's break down the key elements of project management that are crucial for freelancers:

1. Project Definition
Start by clearly defining the scope, objectives, and deliverables of each project. This means

understanding your client's requirements, goals, and expectations right from the beginning. Clarity at this stage sets the foundation for a successful project.

2. Project Planning

Next, break down the project into manageable tasks and set realistic deadlines for each one. Creating a project schedule or timeline helps you track the progress of your work and ensures that you stay on course.

3. Resource Allocation

Determine the resources you'll need to complete the project, including your time, skills, tools, and any external support. Allocating these resources effectively ensures a smooth workflow and prevents bottlenecks.

4. Communication

Establish open and regular communication channels with your clients. Keep them informed about the project's progress, address any challenges that arise, and seek their feedback throughout the process. Good communication is key to managing expectations and building trust.

5. Risk Management

Identify potential risks or obstacles that may come up during the project and develop strategies to mitigate them. This includes having contingency plans in place and being prepared to adapt to changes or unforeseen circumstances.

6. Quality Control

Ensure that the work you deliver meets the highest standards. Implement quality control measures, such as reviewing and editing your work, seeking feedback from clients, and continuously improving your skills. High-quality work will set you apart from the competition.

Effective Project Management Strategies

To manage your freelance projects effectively, consider implementing the following strategies:

1. Break Down the Project

Divide the project into smaller tasks or milestones. This approach helps you manage your time effectively and allows you to track progress easily.

2. Set Priorities

Identify the most critical tasks and prioritize them. Ensuring that the essential components of the project are completed first helps in maintaining a steady workflow and meeting deadlines.

3. Use Project Management Tools

Utilize project management software or tools to stay organized. These tools can assist in task management, tracking deadlines, and collaborating with clients or team members.

4. Maintain Open Communication
Regularly update your clients about the project's progress and address any concerns or questions they may have. Effective communication helps in managing expectations and building trust.

5. Manage Your Time
Create a schedule or calendar to allocate specific time slots for each task. This helps avoid procrastination and ensures that you meet your deadlines.

6. Track and Analyze Your Progress
Monitor your progress throughout the project and make adjustments as necessary. Regularly review your work to ensure it aligns with the project requirements and your client's expectations.

7. Delegate Tasks When Appropriate
If the project requires additional expertise or resources, consider outsourcing or collaborating with other freelancers. Delegating tasks allows you to focus on your areas of expertise and ensures a successful project completion.

Conclusion

Managing freelance projects requires effective planning, organization, and communication. By adopting project management principles and implementing the strategies mentioned in this chapter, you will be better equipped to manage your projects successfully. Delivering high-quality work within deadlines and exceeding client expectations will enhance your reputation and contribute to the growth of your freelancing business.

By taking these steps, you'll be on your way to becoming a more efficient and successful freelancer, ensuring that each project you undertake is a step forward in your professional journey.

Chapter 8: Delivering High-Quality Freelance Work

Hey there! As a freelancer, delivering top-notch work isn't just a goal—it's a necessity. Building a successful and reputable business hinges on your ability to consistently produce outstanding results. Client satisfaction and those precious word-of-mouth referrals all come down to the quality of your work. So, let's dive into some strategies and tips for delivering high-quality freelance work that not only meets but exceeds your clients' expectations.

Understanding Client Requirements

First things first, understanding your client's requirements is crucial. Before you even begin a project, take the time to thoroughly review the project brief and any supporting documents the client provides. If something seems unclear or ambiguous, don't be shy—ask for clarification. Open communication at this stage is vital. Reach out to the client to discuss their goals, preferences, and any specific details they want to be included in the project. This ensures your work aligns with their vision and helps avoid any potential misunderstandings.

Developing a Detailed Project Plan

Once you're clear on the client's needs, it's time to create a detailed project plan. Think of this as your roadmap to success. Break the project down into smaller, manageable tasks and set realistic deadlines for each stage. This approach keeps you organized and focused throughout the project. You might find it helpful to create a visual timeline or use project management tools to track your progress and manage deadlines effectively. Regularly review and adjust your project plan as needed to accommodate any changes or unforeseen circumstances that may arise.

Committing to Clear Communication

Effective communication is a cornerstone of delivering high-quality freelance work. Keep your client updated on the progress of the project, share drafts for feedback, and address any questions or concerns promptly. Regular check-ins ensure you're on the same page and allow for adjustments or refinements before the final delivery. Be receptive to client feedback and incorporate it into your work whenever possible. This not only demonstrates your dedication to meeting their expectations but also shows your commitment to delivering high-quality results.

Attention to Detail and Quality Control

When it comes to delivering high-quality freelance work, attention to detail is paramount. Pay close attention to grammar, spelling, formatting, and overall accuracy. Thoroughly proofread your work before submission to eliminate any errors or inconsistencies. Besides proofreading, conduct a quality control check on your work. Review the project requirements and ensure that your deliverables align with the client's initial vision. Check for any missing elements or areas that may require further refinement.

Meeting Deadlines

In the freelance world, meeting deadlines is non-negotiable. It demonstrates professionalism, reliability, and respect for your client's time. Always strive to deliver your work on or before the agreed-upon deadline. If you encounter any challenges that might delay your progress, communicate this to your client as soon as possible and propose a revised timeline. Transparency and proactive communication are key to maintaining trust and managing client expectations.

Going the Extra Mile

If you really want to stand out and deliver exceptional freelance work, consider going the extra mile. Look for opportunities to add value to your deliverables by exceeding the client's expectations. This could involve providing additional suggestions, recommendations, or insights that enhance the overall quality of the work. Anticipating and addressing potential challenges or questions before they arise shows your dedication to delivering a comprehensive and polished final product.

Conclusion

Delivering high-quality freelance work is essential for building a reputable business and attracting high-quality clients. By understanding client requirements, developing detailed project plans, committing to clear communication, paying attention to detail and quality control, meeting deadlines, and going the extra mile, you can ensure that your freelance work stands out in a competitive market. Strive for excellence in every project you undertake, and you'll establish a strong reputation as a reliable and talented freelancer.

Chapter 9: Building Client Relationships and Generating Referrals

Building strong client relationships is vital for the success and growth of your freelancing business. Satisfied clients not only lead to repeat business and valuable referrals but also contribute significantly to your professional reputation and credibility. In this chapter, we'll explore strategies for building lasting client relationships and generating those all-important referrals.

Understanding Client Needs and Expectations

The foundation of strong client relationships lies in understanding your clients' needs and expectations. Start by having thorough discussions at the beginning of each project. Clarify objectives, deliverables, and timelines to ensure you have a deep understanding of their requirements. By positioning yourself as a reliable and trusted partner, you can set the stage for a successful collaboration.

Effective Communication

Clear and open communication is the cornerstone of successful client relationships. Regularly update your clients on project progress, address any concerns promptly, and be transparent about any challenges or delays. Make sure you are accessible and responsive to their inquiries, and provide regular status updates. By fostering effective communication, you build trust and establish yourself as a dependable freelancer.

Exceeding Client Expectations

One of the most powerful ways to build long-term relationships is by consistently exceeding client expectations. Go the extra mile by delivering high-quality work that surpasses what they anticipated. Always meet deadlines and consistently provide exceptional customer service. This approach not only creates a positive impression but also increases the likelihood of repeat business and referrals.

Nurturing Client Relationships

Building strong and lasting client relationships requires ongoing nurturing and maintenance. Here are some strategies to consider:

Regular Check-ins

Regularly checking in with your clients helps maintain communication and strengthen the relationship. Schedule periodic calls or meetings to discuss ongoing or potential projects, provide updates, and gather feedback. These check-ins also offer an opportunity to understand any changing needs or expectations.

Personalized Approach

Take the time to understand your clients' preferences and tailor your interactions accordingly. Treat each client as an individual and personalize your communication to their specific needs and style. Showing genuine interest and adaptability fosters a stronger connection and builds trust.

Continued Support

Client support doesn't end when the project is complete. Offer ongoing assistance even after the project is finished. This could include answering follow-up questions or providing additional guidance. By being available and supportive, you can solidify the relationship and position yourself as a trusted advisor.

Generating Referrals

Referrals are a powerful way to grow your freelancing business. Satisfied clients are more likely to refer you to their network, providing you with valuable word-of-mouth marketing. Here are some strategies for generating referrals:

Deliver Exceptional Work

The foundation of generating referrals is consistently delivering exceptional work. When clients are delighted with your services, they are more likely to recommend you to others. Focus on quality and exceed expectations to increase your chances of receiving referrals.

Ask for Referrals

Don't be shy about asking your satisfied clients for referrals. After completing a successful project, consider politely requesting referrals. Let them know that you appreciate their support and that referrals are an important part of your business growth. By proactively asking for referrals, you can maximize your chances of receiving them.

Incentivize Referrals

Consider offering incentives to clients who refer you to others. This could be in the form of discounts on future services, exclusive content, or other perks. Incentivizing referrals creates additional motivation for clients to actively promote your services.

Utilize Online Platforms

Leverage online platforms such as freelancer

directories or peer-to-peer recommendation websites to expand your reach and increase your chances of receiving referrals. Create compelling profiles and showcase your expertise and past successes. Encourage satisfied clients to leave reviews and ratings to enhance your credibility and visibility.

Network and Collaborate

Networking and collaborating with other professionals in your industry can lead to valuable referrals. Attend industry events, join online communities, and engage with like-minded professionals. Building relationships with others increases the likelihood of receiving and giving referrals.

Conclusion

Building client relationships and generating referrals are critical components of establishing a successful freelancing business. By understanding client needs, maintaining effective communication, delivering exceptional work, nurturing relationships, and actively seeking referrals, you can position yourself as a trusted and reputable freelancer. Remember, satisfied clients are not only valuable for repeat business but also serve as powerful advocates for your services through referrals.

Chapter 10: Scaling Your Freelancing Business

Scaling your freelancing business is an exciting journey that involves growing and expanding your operations to handle more clients, projects, and revenue. It's a phase that can significantly boost your profitability and success. However, scaling requires careful planning and strategic decisions to ensure a smooth transition while maintaining the quality of your work. In this chapter, we will explore various strategies and considerations for scaling your freelancing business effectively.

1. Evaluate Your Current Business

Before you can scale your freelancing business, it's crucial to assess your current operations and identify areas for improvement. Start by asking yourself a few critical questions:

- Are you consistently reaching full capacity with your current workload?
- Are you efficiently managing your time and resources?
- Have you identified any bottlenecks or areas of inefficiency in your processes?
- Are your services in high demand?
- Do you have a steady stream of clients and projects?

By critically evaluating your business, you can gain insights into its strengths and weaknesses. This self-assessment will help you make informed decisions about where and how to expand.

2. Streamline Your Processes

Effective process management is key to scaling your business successfully. Begin by analyzing your workflow and identifying repetitive or time-consuming tasks that could be automated or outsourced. This will free up your time to focus on high-value activities and increase productivity.

Consider implementing project management tools, time-tracking software, and other automation tools to streamline your processes. These tools can help you track project progress, manage deadlines, collaborate with clients and team members, and analyze project profitability.

3. Expand Your Service Offerings

Diversifying your services can help you attract a broader range of clients and increase your revenue potential. Look for opportunities to leverage your existing skills and expertise to offer additional services within your niche or in complementary areas.

For example, if you are a freelance graphic

designer specializing in logo design, you could expand your services to include branding packages, web design, or social media graphics. This allows you to cater to a wider range of client needs and increase your earning potential.

4. Hire and Delegate

As your business grows, you may reach a point where you can no longer handle all the workload on your own. Hiring and delegating tasks to other freelancers or virtual assistants can help you scale your business effectively. Identify areas where you can outsource tasks that are not core to your expertise or require less specialized skills. This allows you to focus on high-value activities while ensuring that client projects are completed efficiently.

Remember to carefully vet and onboard freelancers to maintain the quality of work and client satisfaction.

5. Build a Team

Scaling your freelancing business may eventually require you to build a team of talented professionals. Consider partnering with other freelancers or hiring employees who can contribute to the growth and success of your business. By building a team, you can handle larger and more complex projects, expand your service offerings, and provide a wider range of expertise to your clients.

However, be mindful of the additional responsibilities and challenges that come with managing a team, such as effective communication, project coordination, and maintaining a positive work culture.

6. Invest in Marketing

Scaling your business also requires attracting a steady stream of new clients. Invest in marketing strategies that align with your target audience and help you stand out in a competitive market. Consider leveraging digital marketing techniques, such as content marketing, social media advertising, search engine optimization (SEO), and email marketing.

Create a strong online presence through a professional website, blog, and social media channels to showcase your expertise and attract potential clients.

7. Focus on Client Retention

While attracting new clients is essential for growth, don't forget the importance of nurturing existing client relationships. Repeat business and referrals from satisfied clients can significantly contribute to the scalability of your freelancing business. Maintain open lines of communication, consistently deliver high-quality work, and provide exceptional customer service to cultivate long-term client relationships.

Offer loyalty programs, special discounts, or exclusive benefits to incentivize repeat business.

8. Continuous Learning and Improvement

To stay competitive and adapt to changing market trends, it's essential to invest in your professional development. Continuously update your skills, stay informed about industry advancements, and seek opportunities to learn and grow. Attend relevant workshops, conferences, and webinars. Join professional networks, industry associations, and online communities to connect with other freelancers and gain valuable insights.

By staying ahead of the curve, you can position yourself as an expert in your niche and attract high-value clients.

Conclusion

Scaling your freelancing business requires careful planning, strategic decision-making, and ongoing evaluation. By evaluating your current business, streamlining processes, expanding service offerings, hiring and delegating, building a team, investing in marketing, focusing on client retention, and continuously learning, you can successfully scale your freelancing business and achieve long-term growth and profitability.

www.ingramcontent.com/pod-product-compliance
Lightning Source LLC
Chambersburg PA
CBHW071221240526
45470CB00018B/2097